Loma Prieta

Francisco X. Alarcón

PS
3551
.L235
L66
1990

ISBN   0-9627192-1-8

Cover photograph by Frank Balthis depicts crack in pavement on the
road up to Loma Prieta, October 19, 1989

Some of these poems first appeared as *Quake Poems*
(Santa Cruz, CA: We Press, 1989), in an effort by the author and
Christopher Funkhouser to raise Earthquake Relief funds.

We Press
POBox 1503 Santa Cruz California 95061

Third Printing, 2000

We Press
62 Westervelt Avenue
Staten Island NY 10301
wepress@con2.com

Contents

To those who lost their lives on October 17, 1989

Introduction

On October 17, 1989, while people sitting in their living rooms all over the world watched in full color our grief and horror, we sat surrounded by darkness and silence with no more protection than one another's arms. When electrical power was finally restored, we saw steel and concrete structures crushed as if stepped on by colossal feet. We shared in the agony of those who waited by collapsed buildings and freeways for news about their missing loved ones. For the next seventy-two hours racial, cultural and social differences were of no consequence, as we reached out to aid one another.

In this extraordinary collection *Loma Prieta*, Francisco X. Alarcón has captured all the elements that make an earthquake such a terrifying event, the contradictory feelings people usually experience during and after such a disaster, and the indomitable energy that makes the human spirit endure.

In a zig-zag motion, characteristic of an earthquake, we journey between the intersecting circles of a physical and a mystical world. We emerge again at the point of departure with a renewed "vision" of the universe within us.

In "Gatherers," the Aztec prophecy that foretells the ending of the Fifth Sun, our present era, on the day 4-earthquake looms in our consciousness, more ominous with every aftershock:

*each
aftershock
brought us
closer
and closer...*

*in hours
we went
back maybe
a thousand
years*

*we were
now
a small band
of mystic
gatherers*

There are constant reminders that technology is useless against the power of nature, bringing into focus once again that our survival depends on our willingness to watch over each other and over the planet we share. In "First Person Eulogy"

> strangers became
> familiar: this pronoun
> "I" for once included
> each and every one

And in "Blessed The Big One," the cataclysm might make it possible for us

> to find a way
> to heal ourselves
> to let
> Earth
> breathe a little

In a number of poems, cities and other physical structures are personified or rehumanized. In "Santa Cruz," for instance, a wounded community regains consciousness

> still feeling
> the missing limbs
> of her amputated
> downtown

Visually minimal but deep like the earth's faults themselves, the poems in the *Loma Prieta* collection are as essential as our need to experience and express love. Indeed, these poems attest to our capacity for loving, for preserving and celebrating life even in the face of cataclysmic obliteration.

Now, let the poems tell you.

Lucha Corpi
Oakland, California

LOMA PRIETA

¿quién
te mordió
las chiches
Madre?

who dared
to bite
your nipples
Mother?

7

MEMORIAL

*"The Pacific Garden Mall
as we know it, ceased to exist
at 5:04 today,"* Mardi Wormhoudt,
Mayor of Santa Cruz, October 17, 1989

do towns
suffer
like people
heartattacks

do buildings
get scared
too and try
to run

do steel
frames
get twisted
out of pain

do windows
break
because
they can't cry

do walls let
themselves go
just
like that

and lie on
sidewalks
waiting
to be revived

is this how
old places
give birth
to new places?

QUAKE EMBRACES

with each
aftershock
we embraced

our arms:
thick roots
searching
for soil

CHANCE

the city
has no
electricity

"what
a nightmare!"
I say

"a chance
to count
stars"

you say
pointing
to the sky

OPORTUNIDAD

la ciudad
no tiene
electricidad

"¡qué
pesadilla!"
digo yo

"una oportunidad
para contar
estrellas"

dices tú
apuntando
al cielo

amor mío
que tus manos
me desentierren
que tus besos
me revivan

que me mojen
tus ojos
que me cubran
tus caricias
y tu vaho

que mi pecho
sienta
el latido de
tu corazón
y tu furia

que todavía
muerda
en la boca
tu flor
y tu esencia

que muerto
siga mirando
tu rostro
que tu cuerpo
sea mi tumba

que quede así
víctima del
terremoto
del amor
y la pasión

DIALECTICA DEL AMOR

para el mundo
no somos nada
pero aquí juntos
tú y yo
somos el mundo

DIALECTS OF LOVE

to the world
we are nothing
but here together
you and I
are the world

GATHERERS

to Sue, Fredy, Little Marisela,
Chris, Cruz, Jaime, and Javier

in front of
our house
we formed
a circle of
chairs

we waited
for the night
listening
to news
on the radio

each
aftershock
brought us
closer
and closer

sometimes
we stared
at each other
sometimes
we laughed

in hours
we went
back maybe
a thousand
years

we were
now
a small band
of mystic
gatherers

BOUNCED CHECK

there is
a crack on
the plaster
beside
my door

a strange
signature
that wrote
a bad check
on my wall

AFTERMATH

next
morning
sadness

turned
into
dust

people
left
foot

prints
crossing
streets

POBRES POETAS

a Miguel Angel Flores

por las calles
rondan poetas
como pajaritos
caídos del nido

dan con los postes
del alumbrado
que de pronto
les salen al paso

ceremoniosos
les piden permiso
a las bancas vacías
de los parques

nadie sabe
ni ellos mismos
por qué les brotan
en los hombros alas

un día quizá usen
por fin esa llave
que desde siempre
traen en el bolsillo

POOR POETS

to Miguel Angel Flores

poets walk aimlessly
on the streets
like chicks fallen
from their nest

they bump into
light posts
that suddenly
cross their path

ceremoniously
they ask permission
from empty benches
in the parks

nobody knows
not even themselves
why wings sprout
from their shoulders

maybe one day finally
they'll use that key
they always carry
inside a pocket

MODERN QUAKE

FAX
delivered

sender:
unknown

FIRE

no camera
can ever
capture

the screams
of a house
on fire

the scent
of so many
memories

dinners
laughter
gone up

in smoke

TREES

also
spoke

fallen
leaves:

their
murmurs

FLOWERS

best
poems
around

LONG LINES

Shopper's
Corner Mart
was
like going
to the movies

ODD HOLIDAY

like on
Memorial
weekend

barbecues
mushroomed
everywhere

MEDIA REALITY

my brother
calls
from Texas

"you guys
are
on TV"

the Marina
the Cypress
Freeway

the Bay Bridge
the Garden
Mall

chopped
images:
just fiction

between beer
and soap
commercials

SAN ANDREAS

every
body's
fault

RELIEF LOGIC

if rich
prompt
relief

no relief
in sight
if poor   `

;

FEMA

(Federal
Emergency
Management
Agency)

another
four
letter
word

would it be better
to never get
power back

to have idle
fridges TV sets
microwave ovens

to never again
run rivers
inside plumbing

would it make
a difference
to let cars rust

to walk around
to ride bikes
instead of freeways

would it give us
at least a chance
to find a way

to heal ourselves
to let Earth
breathe a little

how many trees
how many animals
how many of us

wouldn't give thanks
for being saved
by the Big One

es triste
ser vaso
y nunca
llenarse

ser puerta
y siempre
quedarse
trancada

ser cama
sentirse
mortaja
no lecho

es triste
ser uno
y nunca
sumar dos

ser ave
sin nido
ser santo
sin vela

ser solo
y vivir
soñando
abrazos

how sad
to be a glass
and never
be filled

a door
and stay
always
locked up

a bed
that's
a deathbed
not a nest

how sad
to be oneself
and never
add up to two

a bird
without a nest
a saint
without a candle

to be alone
and live
dreaming
embraces

I lost my home
my china my store
I broke my arm
the back of my neck

I didn't know
what to do
I ran I froze
I cried I laughed

I thought about
the children
I panicked I prayed
I was helpless

I saw the eyes
of the woman
buried at Ford's
I saw myself dying

I was so worried
I felt guilty
I didn't sleep
I snored

I waited and waited
and he never came
I ate all the cookies
I lost my appetite

I read all the papers
I was bored I missed
school I didn't give a damn
about the World Series

I volunteered myself
I overcharged for water
and ice   what the hell
I was rude I was generous

I wrote lots of letters
I finished my projects
I was glued to the TV
I got drunk I got high

I cleaned my room
I was hungry I was cold
I was sad I was angry
I ached all over

I was the looter
and the fireman
I was the preacher
and the hooker

the politician
the grabber of
headliners and
just another loner

I was the dreamer
the listener
the heart-broken
the mouth-piece

strangers became
familiar: this pronoun
"I" for once included
each and every one

PASSAGE

there is
a crack in
every person

as deep as
the deepest
fault on earth

a split
that marks
a leap in wisdom

a wound
that never
really heals

a passage
to the universe
inside each of us

SANTA CRUZ

she wakes up
shivering in
the middle
of the night

still feeling
the missing limbs
of her amputated
downtown

COOPER HOUSE

Santa Cruz Landmark Wrecked
October 26, 1989

like my
grandmother
she was stern
she was proud
she stood in the way

like my
grandmother
she was taken away:
she'll come back
in my sleep

streets
were
repaved

cracked
walls
redone

all
failures
removed

stores
opened
promptly

with
big
smiles

(nothing
happened
here

business
as
usual)

QUAKE UPHEAVALS

in Watsonville as in Managua,
Mexico City and San Salvador

under
their own
weight

power
structures
collapsed

steel
cement
no match

for under
ground
fury

conceiving
a new
order

on tent
camps
people

homeless
hungry
enraged

TAMBORES

*to Javier Muñiz, Raúl Rivera, José Luis Pérez
y toda la palomilla drumming at Fort Mason,
December 15, 1989*

bring us
our ancient
roots

the language
of lakes
and birds

our first
breath
of fire

teach us
the song
of the sea

let us
see with
our hands

touch again
el ombligo
de la tierra

30

CANTO

loma prieta
niña inquieta
sierra herida
loma viva

loma todo
loma nada
alma y pena
loma poema

fuerza prieta
agua honda
hierba dueña
madre grande

loma estrella
ola
    ballena
        mar

loma
  paloma
      abuela
¿ontás?

VISION

to Christopher Funkhouser

there were
no houses
no streets
no fences

only pines
and meadows
tall grasses
and seagulls

on the same
spot where
my bed
once stood

there was
a sea lion
winking
an eye